YOUR KNOWLEDGE HAS VALUE

- We will publish your bachelor's and master's thesis, essays and papers

- Your own eBook and book - sold worldwide in all relevant shops

- Earn money with each sale

Upload your text at www.GRIN.com
and publish for free

Bibliographic information published by the German National Library:

The German National Library lists this publication in the National Bibliography; detailed bibliographic data are available on the Internet at http://dnb.dnb.de .

This book is copyright material and must not be copied, reproduced, transferred, distributed, leased, licensed or publicly performed or used in any way except as specifically permitted in writing by the publishers, as allowed under the terms and conditions under which it was purchased or as strictly permitted by applicable copyright law. Any unauthorized distribution or use of this text may be a direct infringement of the author s and publisher s rights and those responsible may be liable in law accordingly.

Imprint:

Copyright © 2018 GRIN Verlag
Print and binding: Books on Demand GmbH, Norderstedt Germany
ISBN: 9783668709904

This book at GRIN:

https://www.grin.com/document/426458

Chien Duong

The Implications regarding the Effects of explicit an implicit Instruction on linguistic pragmatic Development for vietnamese EFL Students

GRIN Verlag

GRIN - Your knowledge has value

Since its foundation in 1998, GRIN has specialized in publishing academic texts by students, college teachers and other academics as e-book and printed book. The website www.grin.com is an ideal platform for presenting term papers, final papers, scientific essays, dissertations and specialist books.

Visit us on the internet:

http://www.grin.com/

http://www.facebook.com/grincom

http://www.twitter.com/grin_com

The Implications Regarding the Effects of Explicit and Implicit Instruction on Linguistic Pragmatic development for Vietnamese EFL University Students

Authors

Anh Chien Duong

Author Biographies

Anh Chien Duong is a Lecturer in the Department of Foreign Languages, The People's Police Academy of Vietnam. He received a PhD at the University of Newcastle, Australia in 2016. His research interest includes Pragmatic transfer and Pragmatics in language teaching. He has 10 years experience in teaching English and training EFL teachers in Vietnam.

Abstract

In recent years, a considerable scholarly literature has accumulated regarding the most effective techniques for EFL students to develop what is termed, 'pragmatic linguistic competency'. Because the concept of 'pragmatic linguistic competency' represents a notion that is somewhat obscurely defined as 'the capacity to use English language appropriately in spontaneous speaking contexts', the latitude for ambivalent interpretation is more common than we believe it should be. Part of our purpose in this paper is to relieve at least some of the resultant ambiguity surrounding this definition by reconceptualising it in the context of the current pedagogic debate which differentiates two EFL approaches to pragmatic linguistic competency. Both heuristic approaches have come to feature prominently within this framework. These techniques or approaches have become known as 'explicit' and 'implicit' instructional pedagogies. We argue that the explicit pragmatic language acquisition process signifies learning environments in which the learner is introduced to a range of explicitly relevant rules. These rules are reckoned to be interpretively foundational to the form of linguistic constructions required, in the sense that these rules function as a coherent combinatory set. On the other hand, the heuristic of implicit pedagogy "makes no overt reference to rules or forms" (Doughty, 2007, p.265), but only to forms of speech that depend upon rule-governed pragmatics, whose logical structures are to be discovered as students manipulate them, more or less skillfully, during their actual participatory contributions to the conversational exchange. Our objective in this paper will be concerned to diminish the ambivalence which characterises the interpretation of pragmatic linguistic competency by providing a more comprehensive and coherent conceptual scheme for its linguistic deployment.

Key words: pragmatics, pragmatic competence, refusal, explicit, implicit

Introduction

Pragmatics is considered as the ability to use language appropriately in a given context, to understand what speakers really mean when they say something. In deed, people do not always say what they mean. For this reason, even though an EFL learner knows the meaning of a sentence, it is inadequate for him or her to determine what a speaker means in a certain language setting of utterance. A simple example is This table is dirty. Semantically, the word this table means a specific table, dirty means unclean. However, under various circumstances, the speaker might: report the hearer that the table is dirty; tell the hearer to clean up the table;

convince the hearer that the table is dirty; recommend the hearer to take another table… As such, the hearer's failure to comprehend the speaker's intended meaning may cause misunderstandings and lead to conversation breakdowns, or what is termed 'pragmatic failure'(Liu, 2007)

Research on pragmatic acquisition over the pastfew decades has experienced a reproduction of experimental studies concerning the effectiveness of instructional intervention in EFL and ESL classrooms in order to foster learners' ability of pragmatic competence and avoid pragmatic failure(see Ishihara and Cohen, 2010 for comprehensive reviews; Liu, 2007). In line with these generalobjectives of the communication language acquisition, a debate has emerged a pedagogicaldifferences between the two approaches which are considered to be the two most dominant, namely 'explicit' and 'implicit'. In general, the former involves all types of rules which are explained to learners, or when learners are directed to find rules by attending to forms. Conversely, the latter makes no overt reference to rules or forms(Doughty, 2005).

The aims of the present study will be first to consult the relevant literature in order to cater a coherent comprehensive account of each of these instructional interventions. Then the second objective will be to critically evaluate the currentdebate that to a large extent separate the relationship between explicit and implicit instruction, as they are represented by whatProfessor Ronald Laura has termed 'exclusive disjunction'. The scope of this conventional debate thus limited by the logical form of a question raisedby the traditional debate, namely either approach is clearly effective teaching process for language acquisition, i.e. if one method is proved to be effective, then the other is deemed excluded. The purpose of this study will be to show that the nature of the debate itself is structured in a limitedsense and therefore does not do justice to one ofthe approaches to language learning acquisition.The aim of this study will be to spectacle the limited scope of the debate, and then make it wider and more comprehensive.

The above findings have led the researchers to argue for a greater emphasis on pragmatics in L2 classroom (Kondo, 2008; Ishihara and Cohen, 2010). Recently, there have been an increasing number of researches dealing with the effect of instruction on L2 pragmatics learning (Ishihara and Cohen, 2010). Although previous studies have shown that pragmatics is teachable, the issues of whether pragmatic instruction makes a difference; whether there are different effects for different teaching approaches still questionable.

This leads to another central issue discussed extensively in the recent literature on the teaching of L2 pragmatic knowledge is the teaching approaches used in instructions. Generally, in a fair amount of research, explicit instruction may produce more effects than implicit instruction(Soler, 2005; Schmidt, 1990; Nguoi-Lao-Dong, 2012; Hudson et al., 1992, 1995). However, as warned by Hudson (2001), due to a limited number of studies that have investigated the implicit instruction and methodological issues such as unequal treatment lengths for explicit and implicit instructions and variations in data collection methods, the above findings should be treated with caution. Therefore, in order to gain a deep understanding of the effect of implicit vs. explicit instructions on L2 pragmatics learning, further research is certainly needed (Hudson, 2001;Wannaruk, 2008).

The next part of this paper will be to provide a general view of 'pragmatics competence' with which we will be working on.

Pragmatic Competence

Pragmatic Competence refers to the ability to use language appropriately in different social situations. Based on Bachman (1990), pragmatic competence in the present study is defined as the knowledge that learners use to perform a speech act successfully when communicating with native speakers of the target language. It consists of the knowledge of the linguistic resources needed to realize a speech act, of socio-cultural constraints on the use of these linguistic resources, and of sequential aspects of the given speech act.

Why teach pragmatics

For the past few decades, although pragmatics has not received rapt attention it needs in one place or another, linguists and language teachers have been aware of the importance of pragmatic competence in foreign language development and instruction. Research has also revealed that pragmatic competence does not necessarily develop parallel to lexico-grammatical proficiency (Kasper, 2001;Soler, 2005). In fact, "learners often develop grammatical competence in the absence of concomitant pragmatic competence" (Bardovi-Harlig and Dornyei, 1998, p.233), which may lead to a certain degree of communicative failure on high intermediate and even advanced proficiency levels. Thus, imparting knowledge about and raising awareness of pragmatic aspects and strategies(Bardovi-Harlig and Griffin, 2005; Ghobadi and Fahim, 2009), providing opportunities for output and practice (VanPatten, 2003; Fukuya and Martinez-Flor, 2008) need to be central features of successful FL teaching.

To achieve these goals, classroom instruction is necessary in the way that makes language available to learners for observation. Indeed, even in an L2 setting, if teachers fail to create the target environment or provide students with the input they need, students may not make use of what pragmatic information they possess or know already. That may always be the case in EFL environment where there is usually insufficient access to the target language. Thus, by providing authentic input through formal instruction, teachers can engage learners into the learning of pragmatics.

What is more, teaching pragmatics deserves advocate due to the fact that learners show significant difference from native speakers in terms of language use, the execution and comprehension of certain speech acts, in conversational functions such as greetings and leave takings. As non-native speakers, they do not know the similarities or differences in the target language. Research findings reveal that either they not aware of them, they fail to recognize them, they cannot distinguish them, or simply ignore them, depending on the given contexts where non-native speakers are tested. That does not mean they do not know what to do but that they do not do it because they lack experience or awareness of what is expected from them. This is a valid reason to confirm that pragmatics should be taught. Hence, instruction facilitates students to understand the rules, the pragmatic difference between their native culture and the target one, raise their awareness of what is and is not appropriate in given contexts. AsKasper (1997) put it, "without some form of instruction, many aspects of pragmatic competence do not develop sufficiently."

Classroom instruction also provides a safe place for learners to learn and experiment. In the classroom setting, learners have an opportunity to try out new forms and patterns of communication in an accepting environment.

Pragmatic Failure in Vietnam Context

Pragmatic failure, or pragmatic transfer occurs when learners transfer first language pragmatic rules into foreign/second language domains. In other words, Thomas mentioned pragmatic failure as "...the inability to understand 'what is meant by what is said' " (Thomas, 1983, p.91; see also Yuan, 2012 for a review). The term 'failure' is somehow different from "error" because 'what is said' may not be incorrect, but cannot reach the speaker's communicative intention. For that reason, even if an EFL learner is enable to speak fluently, inappropriate speech may cause him or her to appear unintentionally rude, uncultured or awkward (Amaya, 2008).

This seems to be the case for Vietnamese EFL learners in general and the English majors in particular. After years of learning English, they are still lack of pragmatic competence, whichencompasses speech acts, conversational structure, discourse organization, and sociolinguistic aspects of language use such as choice of address forms, and is generallyunderstood as "knowledge of the sequential aspects of speech acts,...the appropriate contextual use of the particular language's linguistic resources" (Barron, 2003, p.10). Due to the lack of pragmatic competence, not many Vietnamese major EFL learners have the ability to realize the nuance of speech act strategies in English (Huong, 2012). In her study, Huong (2012) concludes that 63% major EFL Vietnamese students fail to perform English pragmatics (request) appropriately, even though they use a polite request strategy in their native language. This leads to the misinterpretation of the message conveyed. She also illustrates pragmatic failure of Vietnamese major EFL learners in her situation that a group leader asks members in the group to meet for a rehearsal of the oral presentation:

Can you go to Nhung's to have a rehearsal at 2 pm tomorrow?

This request sounds strange to English native speakers, and sometimes it is considered as rude. In fact, the speaker transfers a common Vietnamese request "Các bạn có thể đến nhà Nhung để tập duyệt vào ngày mai lúc 2 giờ không?" to a structurally equivalent utterance. The speaker is not aware that his use of indirect request distances him from other members of the group not to mention the risk that he may suffer from a refusal (Huong, 2012, p.79).

This is consistent with other relevant research findings, which attribute the difference in making English refusal strategies by non-native speakers to the lack of pragmatic competence (Phuong, 2006; Beebe et al., 1990; Silva, 2003;Bardovi-Harlig and Griffin, 2005; Ishihara and Cohen, 2010). Indeed, although equipped with linguistic skills, i.e. listening skill, speaking skill, reading skill, writing skill, and even British and American culture, many Vietnamese major EFL learners still find it difficult in comprehending or conveying the intended intentions and politeness values (Huong, 2012). As a result, they are still unable to communicate effectively in many situations and contexts, and to control a wide range of language functions, which are how speakers use language for requesting, apologizing, complaining, and promising, among others.

The importance of pragmatics is also emphasized by Cohen (2010):

"Having pragmatic ability means being able to go beyond the literal meaning of what is said or written, in order to interpret the intended meanings, assumptions, purposes or goals, and the kinds of actions that are being performed" (p.5)

For this reason, it is necessary to understand and create language that is appropriate to the situations in which one is functioning, because failure to do so may cause users to miss key points that are being communicated or to have their message misunderstood (Kondo, 2008).

In the context of teaching, the aim of teaching pragmatics is to facilitate the learners' sense of being able to find socially appropriate language for the situations that they encounter (Kathleen, 2006). Despite being aware of the importance of pragmatic in language teaching, most VietnameseEFL teachers still do not know what is included in teaching pragmatics (Huong, 2012). They still seems to be confused in choosing the teaching methods for pragmatics and do not know which method will provide the most effective.

Explicit and Implicit Instruction

Over the past few decades, research on pragmatic acquisition has experienced a reproduction of experimental studies concerning the effectiveness of instructional intervention in EFL and ESL classrooms in order to foster learners' ability of pragmatic competence and avoid pragmatic failure(see Ishihara and Cohen, 2010 for comprehensive reviews; Liu, 2007). In line with these generalobjectives of the communication language acquisition, a debate has emerged a pedagogicaldifferences between the two approaches which are considered to be the two most dominant, namely 'explicit' and 'implicit'.

In general, explicit and implicit instruction do not correlate exactly with direct and indirect intervention, but can be mapped onto it (Ellis, 2009). Explicit instruction includes all types of which rules are explained to learners, or when learners are directed to find rules by attending to forms. Conversely, implicit instruction makes no overt reference to rules or forms (Doughty, 2005). In other word, implicit instruction involves learners in inferring the rule without their attention being directly focused on it. Housen and Pierrard (2005) describe a more detailed definition of the two types of instruction in terms of a number of differentiating characteristics, as shown in Table 1 below:

Table 1: Implicit and explicit instruction(Housen and Pierrard, 2005)

Implicit	Explicit
Attracts attention to target form	Directs attention to target form
Is delivered spontaneously (e.g. in an otherwise communication-oriented activity)	Is predetermined and planned (e.g. as the main focus and goal of a teaching activity)
Is unobtrusive (minimal interruption of communication of meaning)	Is obtrusive (interruption of communicative meaning)
Presents target forms in context	Presents target forms in isolation
Makes no use of metalanguage	Uses metalinguistic terminology (e.g. rule explanation)
Encourages free use of the target form	Involves controlled practice of target form

The Exclusive Disjunctional Debate in Explicit/Implicit Studies

Previous research on the effects of pragmatic instruction can be categorized into two groups regarding the nature of input: explicit instruction versus no instruction, and explicit instruction versus implicit instruction (see Kasper & Rose, 1999; Takahashi, 2010 for comprehensive reviews).

In the first category, studies show a large advantage for explicit instruction over no instruction (Takimoto, 2006; Takahashi and Beebe, 1987; Hudson, 2001; Kondo, 2001). Kondo (2001) applied a pre-test/post-test design to explore whether learners' use of refusal strategies changed after explicit instruction and what pragmatic aspects the learners became more aware of through explicit instruction. The study was carried out on thirty-five Japanese L2 learners of English. The instructional treatment on American refusals consists of implicit/explicit teaching including explicit explanation and analysis of semantic formulas, controlled free practices and cross-cultural comparison followed by discussion. Results showed improvement of the Japanese learners towards the patterns of American refusals.

In the second category, generally, in a fair amount of research, explicit instruction may produce more effects than implicit instruction (Soler, 2005;Schmidt, 1990; Nguoi-Lao-Dong, 2012; Hudson et al., 1992, 1995). Hudson (2001)'s meta-analysis covered 13 ILP instruction studies focusing on a variety of pragmatic features. They found larger average effects for explicit interventions (d = .70) than implicit interventions (d=.44). However, once confidence intervals were taken into account they could not make any substantial claims for the superior benefits of explicit instruction. Nguoi-Lao-Dong (2012)compared explicit instruction on conversational routines with an implicit condition in which learners received input and practice. While she found that, overall, the explicit group learners 'developed a more richly varied, more interpersonally active repertoire of gambit and strategy types and tokens' (Nguoi-Lao-Dong, 2012, p.245), she also discovered that the explicit instruction was not superior for some of the targeted L2 pragmatic features. However, numerous other studies have not found such conclusive differences between explicit and implicit treatments (e.g. Thuy, 2004;Koike and Pearson, 2005; Martinez-Flor and Fukuya, 2005). In all of these studies, both explicit and implicit treatments had stronger effects than a control group. However, the differences between the two treatments were not so clear.

Based on the above review, it can be said that thepurpose of the previous studies is mainly to identify the most effective pragmatic instruction.This conventional debate indicate that the nature ofthe research envolves determining one instruction if premirer than the other. In other words, previous studies have made an attempt to polarize the relationship between explicit and implicit instructional approaches, as if they represented by what Professor Ronald Laura has termed an 'exclusive disjunction'. The scope of the debate is thus limited by the logical form of the very question posed by the traditional debate, namely either the explicit approach is the most effective instructional process for pragmatic language acquisition or the implicit instructional approach is. The limiting factor is the exclusivity of the disjunctional clause; namely if one approach is deemed to be most effective, then the other process is by entailment covertly excluded and marginalized as an effective instructional process. To answer this question in a more comprehensive and holistic way that has yet happened, the current study will apply a new modal created by Professor Laura - 'presuppositional analysis' as a reflection of the expected outcome with the respect of philosophical stand.

Summary and Conclusion

The significance of the study lies in the pedagogical implication, as to the researchers' knowledge, for the first time, of the feasibility of combining both linguistic competence and pragmatic competence for being suitable to Vietnamese language classrooms. The bias toward teaching pragmatic competence in Vietnam is hoped to reduce to some extent. Regarding teaching, in line with Ishihara and Cohen (2010, p.76)'s argument: "If no formal instruction is provided, it is said to generally take at least 10 years in a second- language context to be able to use the language in a pragmatically nativelike manner", and Soler (2005)'s finding: "Different teaching approaches need to be operationalised and implemented taking into account particular educational contexts", it is hoped that this study will prove the need of instruction in teaching pragmatics in Vietnam. A teacher might take a pedagogical transfer from focusing on linguistic performance to focusing on a more pragmatic perspective. As to learning, with the implementation of pragmatic teaching, the study will hopefully raise awareness of Vietnamese learners of English in pragmatic issue, and thus, improving pragmatic competence.

By conducting this study, we hope to determine the extent to which the underlying framework within which the debate has been structured serves to restrict unnecessarily the range of plausible interpretations. In other words, it seems that the framework of the interpretation in the current debate is dualistic.

References

Amaya, L. a. F. n. (2008). Teaching Culture: Is It Possible to Avoid Pragmatic Failure? Revista Alicantina de Estudios Ingleses, 21, 11-24.

Bachman, L. (1990). Fundamental Considerations in Language Testing, Oxford, Oxford University Press.

Bardovi-Harlig, K. & Dornyei, Z. (1998). Do Language Learners Recognize Pragmatic Violations? Pragmatic Versus Grammatical Awareness in Instructed L2 Learning. TESOL Quarterly, 32, 233-262.

Bardovi-Harlig, K. & Griffin, R. (2005). L2 Pragmatic Awareness: Evidence from the ESL Classroom. System, 33, 401- 415.

Barron, A. (2003). Learning how to do things with words in a study abroad context John Benjamins Publishing Company.

Beebe, L. M., Takahashi, T. & Uliss-Weltz, R. (1990). Pragmatics Transfer in ESL Refusals. In:Scarcella, R. C., Andersen, E. S. & Krashen, S. D. (eds.) Developing Communicative COnpetence in a Second Language. Heinle & Heinle Publisher.

Cohen, A. D. (2010). Coming to Terms with Pragmatics. In: Cohen, N. I. A. D. (ed.) Teaching and Learning Pragmatics:Where Language and Culture Meet. Pearson Longman.

Doughty, C. J. (2005). Instructed SLA: Constraints, Compensation, and Enhancement. In:Doughty, C. J. & Long, M. H. (eds.) The Handbook of Second Language Acquisition. Blackwell Publishing.

Ellis, R. (2009). Implicit and Explicit Knowledge in Second Language Learning, Testing and Teaching.In: Singleton, D. (ed.) SECOND LANGUAGE ACQUISITION. Multilingual Matters.

Fukuya, Y. & Martinez-Flor, A. (2008). The Interactive Effects of Pragmatic-Eliciting Tasks and Pragmatic Instruction. Foreign Language Annals,41, 478-500.

Ghobadi, A. & Fahim, M. (2009). The Effect of Explicit Teaching of English 'Thanking Formulas' on Iranian EFL Intermediate Level Students at English Language Institutes. System, 526-537.

Housen, A. & Pierrard, M. (2005). Investigations in Instructed Second Language Acquisition. In:Jordens, P. (ed.) Studies on Language Acquisition.Berlin: Mouton de Gruyter.

Hudson, J. (2001). Indicators for Pragmatic Instruction: some quantitative tools. In: (Eds.), K. R. R. G. K. (ed.) Pragmatics in language teaching.Cambridge, UK: Cambridge University Press.

Hudson, J., Detmer, E. & Brown, J. D. (1992). A framework for testing cross-cultural pragmatics,Honolulu, Second Language Teaching & Curriculum Center, University of Hawai'i at Manoa.

Hudson, J., Detmer, E. & Brown, J. D. (1995).Developing prototypic measures of cross-cultural pragmatics, Honolulu, Second Language Teaching & Curriculum Center, University of Hawai'i at Manoa.

Huong, V. T. L. (2012). Linguistic And Cultural Features of Requests: Some Implications For Teaching And Learning English As A Foreign Language. Journal Of Science, Hue University, 70,71-85.

Ishihara, N. & Cohen, A. D. (2010). Learners' pragmatics: potential causes of divergence. In:Ishihara, N. & Cohen, A. D. (eds.) Teaching and Learning Pragmatics: Where Language and Culture Meet. Pearson Education Limited.

Kasper, G. (1997). Can pragmatic competence be taught? Available:http://www.nflrc.hawaii.edu/NetWorks/NW06/[Accessed 19 May 2013].

Kasper, G. (2001). Classroom research on interlanguage pragmatics. In: Rose, K. R. & Kasper, G. (eds.) Pragmatics in language teaching.Cambridge University Press.

Koike, D. A. & Pearson, L. (2005). The effect of instruction and feedback in the development of pragmatic competence. . System, 33, 481-501.

Kondo, S. (2001). Instructional effects on pragmatic development: Interlanguage refusal.PacSLRF. University of Hawai'i at Manoa.

Kondo, S. (2008). Effects on pragmatic development through awareness-raising instruction: Refusals by Japanese EFL learners. In: (Eds.), E. A. n.-S. A. M. 1.-F. (ed.) Investigating pragmatics in foreign language learning, teaching and testing.Bristol, UK: Multilingual Matters.

Liu, C.-N. (2007). Pragmatics in foreign language instruction: the effects of pedagogical intervention and technology on the development of efl learners' realization of "request". Texas A&M University.

Martinez-Flor, A. & Fukuya, Y. (2005). The effects of instruction on learners' production of appropriate and accurate suggestions. System,33, 463-480.

Nguoi-Lao-Dong. (2012). 929 giao vien tieng Anh chua dat chuan [Online]. Available:http://nld.com.vn/20120522101726160p0c1017/929-giao-vien-tieng-anh-chua-dat-chuan.htm[Accessed January 15.

Phuong, N. T. M. (2006). Cross-cultural pragmatics: Refusals of requests by Australian native speakers of English and Vietnamese learners of English. Ph.D Thesis, The University of Queensland.

Schmidt, R. (1990). The role of conciousness in second language learning. Applied Linguistics, 11,129-58.

Silva, A. J. B. D. (2003). The effect of instruction on pragmatic development: teaching polite refusals in English. Second Language Studies, 55-106.

Soler, E. A. n. (2005). Does instruction work for learning pragmatics in the EFL context? system,33, 417-435.

Takahashi, T. & Beebe, L. M. (1987). The development of pragmatic competence by Japanese learners of English. JALT Journal.

Takimoto, M. (2006). The effects of explicit feedback on the development of pragmatic proficiency. Language Teaching Research, 10,393-417.

Thomas, J. (1983). Cross-cultural Pragmatic Failure. Applied Linguistics. 91-112.

Thuy, T. Q. N. (2004). An investigation into Vietnamese refusal strategies. MA thesis, University of Queensland.

VanPatten, B. (2003). From Input to Output: A Teacher''s Guide to Second Language Acquisition, New York, McGraw-Hill.

Wannaruk, A. (2008). Pragmatic transfer in Thai EFL refusals. RELC Journal, 39, 318-337.

Yuan, Y. (2012). Pragmatics, perceptions and strategies in Chinese college English learning. Ph.D, Queensland University of Technology.

YOUR KNOWLEDGE HAS VALUE

- We will publish your bachelor's and master's thesis, essays and papers

- Your own eBook and book - sold worldwide in all relevant shops

- Earn money with each sale

Upload your text at www.GRIN.com
and publish for free